PhiyahPhlows

Jayne Phlow

PHIYAH PHLOW

PHIYAH PHLOWS

Copyright © 2015 Tiffany Glover

All rights reserved. No part of this book may be reproduced or transmitted in any form or by any means, electronic or mechanical, including photocopying, recording, or by any information storage and retrieval system, without permission in writing from the publisher. All questions and/or request are to be submitted to: 134 Andrew Drive, Reidsville NC, 27320.

To the best of said publisher's knowledge, this is an original manuscript and is the sole property of Author **JAYNE PHLOW.**

Printed in the United States

ISBN-13:978-0692460306
ISBN-10:0692460306

Printed by Createspace 2015
Published by BlaqRayn Publishing 2015

PHIYAH PHLOW

Books by Jayne Phlow

GET A Grip:
Spilled Ink from My Soul

PHIYAH PHLOW

Phiyah Phlows

Jayne Phlow

PHIYAH PHLOW

AGAIN AND AGAIN AND AGAIN AND AGAIN

Animalistic
Cannibalistic
Full court lovin'
Bout to go ball-istic
The aroma of anticipation
Hangs low in the air
Lost in love's intoxication
Please leave me there
The closer I pull up to you
The weaker I get
The electricity in your fingertips
Has me shockingly wet
Heart damn near stops beating
As your lips taste mine
Your hands grip my hips
Commencing this slow wine
The outside world is now irrelevant
It's just us two
Me and you....toe-to-toe
Doing what we came to do
And as we finish round one
Awash in the remains of our rain
Our smiles signify we're both in agreement
Let's crank this shit up again

ALTER EGO

I wish I exuded strength like you
Knew how to command a room like you
Bust in with my head held high
And a domineering twinkle in my eye
And smile despite my fears...like you

I wish I could speak my mind like you
Never worrying whether others see me as
unkind....like you
Knowing I have the right to speak
But as the days go by, I grow ever weak
Why can't I shake it off...like you

It's a shame I have to resort to altering my ego just
to get my points across
People mistaking this fire for a "bitch" persona
when I only want to seen as a "boss"
Words die in my throat soon as I open my
mouth...now I feel awkward and lost

In you, I see every bit of the woman
I was meant to be
So sure of herself, unafraid of being free
You are the woman I want the world to see
So instead of being the reflection in the
mirror...please reflect your soul in me

PHIYAH PHLOW

AND STILL WE DANCE

After all these years, you still make feel as young as
the day we first met
You don't see my hair filled with gray
Nor do you see my varicose veins
You still smile at the way my hips sway

Despite my few aches and pains you continue to
woo me
Bringing me flowers and such
Your fingers still send electric shocks through me
At even the slightest touch

Your silly jokes still make me chuckle
And your kisses still make me melt
The love we make still makes my knees buckle
I've remained the one and only notch in your belt

Our impromptu living room dances
As Billie and Nat croon behind us
Still sends me swingin' as we steal little glances
Losing ourselves in a world where no one can find
us

After all these years, you still call me your "girl"
And I still call you "my guy"
40 years of this dip, this spin, this twirl
You keep me floating on air...I believe I can fly

We're in this thing "til death do we part"
So please God, grant us both long life
So that we may live each day as a brand new start
On our journey as husband and wife

PHIYAH PHLOW

BLACKULATION

So my son and 2 of his friends had the GALL
To be walking to another friend's house the other day
And a cop decided they warranted being stopped
As they journeyed along the way

Were they being obnoxious? Slap-boxing each other?
Perhaps they were making too much noise?
Were they behaving like animals, running wild in the streets?
Or were they acting like normal teenage boys?

It truly doesn't matter what the reason is
Because they've all been out shadowed by ONE fact
That the ONLY thing he noticed as he rolled up on these boys
Is the color of their skin....BLACK

WWB...Walking While Black
Must really be a legitimate crime
And as that cop approached my son and his friends
I can't help but wonder what was really on his mind

Flashing them with his brights, getting out of his car
And shining his flashlight in each face
And no, says my son, he never patted them down
It doesn't matter though...he'd already violated their space

I'm STILL choking on a plethora of emotions
From hurt to utter disgust
Because the ones we were taught to call on for protection

PHIYAH PHLOW

Has now lost EVERY BIT of my trust

Thank God my son tells me that instead of the cop
continuing to harass them
He finally leaves them alone
And all I could do is lift my hands in praise
Because THEY were able come home

And THAT is why we must continue to fight
As we pray and give God all the glory
Our children SHALL be the exception
Rather than the next CNN story..

BLINDED BY THE FACTS

"Wait on the Lord: be of good courage, and He shall strengthen thine heart: wait I say, on the Lord." Psalm 27:14.

What's a logical amount of time to wait on anything?
For example, the bus?
How about a cab?
Or to be seen by the doctor?

Perhaps those particular questions aren't quite logical to ask.
You see, as long as you have the bus schedule,
And you're in the proper place at the proper time,
You ALREADY KNOW that eventually the bus will arrive to take you to your destination.

You called a cab to come pick you up;
And while the cab still hasn't arrived yet,
You're not worried, because your call has been logged and
You ALREADY KNOW that eventually the cab will arrive to take you to your destination.

Your doctor's appointment was at 8am.
It's now 9am and you have yet to be seen.
You probably won't make a fuss though because even though the doctor is running behind,
You ALREADY KNOW that because you've been scheduled to be seen, you SHALL be seen.

The bus hasn't arrived yet.
The cab hasn't pulled up to your door yet.
The doctor STILL hasn't called your name yet.

PHIYAH PHLOW

Yet,
We continue to sit….and wait.
Why?
Because we know that if we are patient,
And continue to wait,
EVENTUALLY, we'll FINALLY receive what we've been waiting on:

The bus will FINALLY pull up to your stop;
The cab will FINALLY blow the horn for you;
And the doctor will FINALLY see you now.

Our waiting FINALLY paid off!
Patience was SHO NUFF a virtue!

Thing is…
It was EASY waiting on those things, right?
Because even though we couldn't SEE them RIGHT THEN,
We maintained our FAITH in the FACT that
No matter HOW long we may have to sit and wait for them,
EVENTUALLY, they SHALL show up, right?

So then….
Why can't we maintain that exact,
Same,
Unwavering FAITH when it comes to waiting on The Lord?
Because right now….
We don't SEE Him.
What we DO see though, are the
COLD,
HARD,
FACTS!

PHIYAH PHLOW

You lost your job.
The bills are due.
The car is acting up.
The chir'en done lost their ever-loving minds.
Ain't no food in the house.
No money coming in to provide.
Your head hurts.
Your back hurts.
Your feet hurt.
Your heart hurts.
Because you're tired.
Tired of watching;
Tired of waiting;
Tired of struggling;
Tired of crying;
Tired of not knowing when change is FINALLY coming.
And,

If you're not afraid to be TOTALLY honest with yourself right now,
You're even tired….of praying.
You're just plain, ol' tired.

But wait a minute now….
Haven't you been in THIS place before?
And hasn't the Lord ALWAYS shown up?
Just like the bus?
Just like the cab?
Just like the doctor?

So then WHY in God's Name are we trippin' when the FACT is
We ALREADY KNOW that the Lord has ALREADY handled EVERYTHANG!

PHIYAH PHLOW

And we are good to go!
We just can't SEE it yet.

So in the meantime,
Pour yourself a nice, cool glass of sweet tea,
Kick your feet up,
And relax.
And get ready.

Because He's already on the way…

BLUE CREAM

Pitch black room
As I lay on my back
Staring up at the painted cracks
Watching the rotation of my ceiling fan
Pissed because once again
I'm allowing myself to fantasize about HIS hands
Dreaming that HIS fingers are dancing among the petals of
My spacious land
I hate him so much
But DAMN his touch
Has my mind hanging in the balance
Of my own personal purgatory
Definitely don't wanna open my heart to him
AGAIN
But is it ok if I open my legs to him
AGAIN
Mmmmm I sure do want him between my legs
AGAIN
I'm having these types a thoughts far too frequently these days
Always coming THIS close to sending him that text
Telling him to come on over and gimme his sex
I mean isn't it true the dick is always better when it comes from
Your ex
Maybe….maybe not….too much of a punk to find out
So I, instead, reach out to another friend of mine
Who I've known for a couple years now
And always treats me just fine
Never tells me no lies
Never makes me cry
Unless of course it's that "Stella Tear"

PHIYAH PHLOW

Escaping the confines of my left eye
I always know where he is
And where he'll always be
Because he doesn't share his lovin' with anybody
But me
So when I need that release
To set my body at ease
I always find him sitting right there waiting for me
In my chest of drawers
In the second drawer
To the left nestled comfortably beneath my draws
I grab hold of my "Boy Blue"
Cuz he never makes me blue
And with a smile I lay on my back…staring up at the painted cracks
Watching the rotation of my ceiling fan
And allow "Blue" to do
Exactly what he was designed to do…

PHIYAH PHLOW

BULLSHIT I BE TELLING MYSELF

Psssshhhh!
Please!
I don't love that nucca no mo'!
How can I actually love somebody that
Played me and
Dogged me out and
Treated me like shit?!
Man fuck that nucca!
Ol' bitch ass!
He will NEVER have the pleasure of even
SNIFFIN' this again!
AAAAAAND if he was here RIGHT NOW,
Standing smack dab in front of my face,
I don't give a flyin fuck
How FINE HE LOOK or
How GOOD HE SMELLS or
How SWOLE HIS SWAG is!
I'd tell his ass
IN my "Martin voice" to

"GETS TA STEPPIN!!"

OHHHHHHH!
So NOOOOOOW we got the NERVE to be calling somebody?!

Hello?
Oh I see we DO know how to dial a number after all.
Oh you've been busy huh?
Mmmm…ok well how about I'm too busy to entertain your ass right now!
What?

PHIYAH PHLOW

Come over here for what?
Nah bruh…
We ain't got shit to discuss IN PERSON
That we can't talk about over the phone.

Silence….
Wait for it….
Wait for it….

Sigh….
Yeah whatever man.
I'll see you when you get here.

Humpf…!
His ass sure got here quick.
Prolly think he gon' get some.
But ALL he gon' get tonight is his
Fuckin feelings hurt.
Damn…
He lookin foine as hell…as usual!
Yeah…
He think he REEEEEAAAL slick.
But he in for a REEEEEAAAL rude awakening
Cuz I ain't the same chick he used to dealin with.
Matter fact…
Lemme get in my "bitch mode" right now!

What the hell is he smilin at?
With his beautiful pearly whites…
Shining like diamonds dipped in sunshine…

Ok does he NOT see this
"I ain't the mutha-fuckin one" look on my face right now?

I HATE when he says my name like that!

PHIYAH PHLOW

Sounding like Barry White…
Mixed with Dennis Haysbert…
Mixed with Idris Elba…
Only better.
Laaaawd ha'mercy!

Wait…who told him to hug me?
NO part of my body language told him to do that…!
Or did it?
Oh.
My.
God….
His chest feels…
And smells…
So…
Fuckin…
Gooooooood!

No girl NO!
You're weakening….
YOU'RE WEAKENING!!!

No I'm not.
This is JUST a hug.
A simple little,
Insignificant,
"Hey how ya doin"
HUG.

Yeeesssss….
A hug that has me wetter than the waters
Phlowing from the Niagara Falls.
But either way….
It's STILL just a hug!

I mean,

PHIYAH PHLOW

Page 15

NOTHING can
Or WILL
Happen off a simple little,
Insignificant,
"Hey ya doin"
Hug….right?

RIGHT….???
Yeah ok…right...

PHIYAH PHLOW

CAN SOMEBODY PLEASE TELL ME WHAT I DID THOUGH?

God is great!
And God is good!
It's such a beautiful day
In my neighborhood!

I just got paid
And I'm feeling fine;
And running a few errands
Is all that's on my mind.

The first thing I do
Is hit the grocery store.
I pay for my items
And as I'm walkin' out the door,

The alarm goes off
And quicker than a sneeze,
Security swarms like bees,
And brings me to my knees.

I'm confused and disoriented
Because it all happened so fast;
They're going through my bags
And counting my cash;

Vehemently searching
For that imaginary "thing" I took;
I side-eye the cashier,
Throwing her a "help me" look.

PHIYAH PHLOW

She ignores my silent plea
And stares through me instead.
And at that moment I truly wish
That I hadn't gotten outta bed.

Now here come the cops;
Them "good ol boys in blue;"
Waving their batons;
Hounding me for the "truth."

But I may as well be speaking a foreign language
Because they hear nothing I say.
So I take a deep breath
And quietly I pray.

And then I figure, "HEY!
I'll just show them my receipt!"
So I dig in my pocket
And in a split heartbeat,

What sounds like a million fireworks
Rips through the air;
I see people running;
I hear screaming;
Wait…what just happened here?

Then suddenly a sharp pain cripples me;
I fall flat on my back;
And as I stare up at the ceiling,
Everything starts going black.

I don't even understand…what did I do wrong?
I only came in for 10 items or less.
So can somebody be kind enough to explain to me
How I ended up with 10 holes in my chest?

PHIYAH PHLOW

From Emmett to Trayvon, to Jordan, Eric and now Michael; from my baby to your baby, and her baby and his baby; ENOUGH really IS E DAMN NOUGH! LEAVE OUR MEN AND BOYS ALONE!!!

#unarmedyetstillconsidereddangerous

PHIYAH PHLOW

CAN SOMEBODY THROW ME A TOWEL PLEASE?

Bills to the left of me; Bills to the right
Water bill
Phone bill
Car insurance
Light
Drowning under grocery bill
Drowning under rent
I tend to keep shit internalized
So forgive me for this vent
Haven't worked in 8 months
Trying hard to survive
Trying hard to remain grateful
Every day I'm still alive
Cuz every day I'm still alive
That's another day to try
But every day I wanna cry
Because my well has gone dry
No need to ask God "why"
Because the answer's always "why not"
I just wanna be able to pay these damn bills and afford to get my child's hair cut
That ain't askin' for a lot
But here I be
Sinking ever deeper in this murky pile of debt
I know my Savior cometh, but I do wish He'd hurry
Because I still don't see my life raft yet...

PHIYAH PHLOW

CHAIN REACTION

I'm not sure how much longer I'll be able
To hold my breath;
Waiting for you to decide to let go of whatever it is
That has you rooted in your shame.
Confined.
Trapped.
Chained.

Why do you refuse to be free?
Then again,
I guess the same can be asked of me.
You see, try as I might to break through the surface,
Bob just a wee bit higher,
Get my head just above water so I can finally
exhale,
I continue to give all my power to the "things" of
this world,
Allowing the weights to pull me back down.

Complacency is so easy, isn't it?
But is it beneficial to our health?
Physically.
Emotionally.
Mentally.
Spiritually.

Because of our individual demons,
Our STRONGHOLDS,
Neither of us can be everything we both possess
The power to be for each other.

You're reaching out your hand to me,
Struggling to save me from the murky swamp of
My misery.

PHIYAH PHLOW

And I hold the key to the one thing that can relinquish you from
Your shackled and shattered past….
My heart.

So on the count of 3,
Let's break these locks and decide
Once and for all,
That even though our pasts were born unto us,
They will never live to dictate our present.

This situation is dire,
And our future is at stake.

It's now…or never…
1…
2…
3…

PHIYAH PHLOW

CHECK YES OR NO

Strawberry Jam
The Queen of Hearts
Tell me the name
Of your sweetheart

Mansion, Apartment, Shack, House
Oh the games we use to play
To help us "pick" our spouse

Imagine if there was any
Kinda truth to this shit
Would we still be passing notes
To the one that we're with?

Making eyes across class
Giggling with my girls when you walk past
Pretending to be mad
When you slap me on my ass

Sneaking on the phone
Soon as my mama goes to sleep
Trying to devise a plan
For a late creep

Your fade is topped off high
And my stone-wash fit tight
And we got crazy prophylactics
To last us through the whole night

Hugging and kissing
And sexing under the moon
Acting grown too soon
Listening to Keith Sweat croon

PHIYAH PHLOW

Professing our love
Promising to "Make It Last Forever"
20 years and 3 kids later
We're fighting to stay together

Baby what happened to us?
I hate how things have changed
We're growing further and further apart
Becoming more and more estranged

What happened to our "teenage love?"
What happened to walks in the park?
What happened to stealing sweet kisses on the swings?
And us "sneaking out" after dark?

We're losing everything that made us US
And I'll do anything to get it back
Starting with these words that I bleed from my heart
As this ink turns my tears jet black

If I had this life to do all over again
And my future was put back on the line
No doubt, I would choose you EVERY single time
Anything else has NEVER crossed my mind

Question is, do you feel the same way?
If you had other options, which direction would you go?
If you had the choice…would you pick me again?
Am I still your "forever?"

Check yes….or no

PHIYAH PHLOW

CINQUAIN POETRY

MY BPC CHALLENGE

The Cinquain poem was developed by poet Adelaide Crapsey in the early 1900's and derives from the French word for five (cinq). There are 2 types of this particular style: the modern cinquain and the traditional cinquain.

The modern cinquain is based on a word count of words of a certain type:

Line 1 has one word (the title).
Line 2 has two words that describe the title.
Line 3 has three "–ing" words that tell the action.
Line 4 has four words that express the feeling
Line 5 has one word which recalls the title.

The traditional cinquain is based on a syllable count which equals a total of 22 syllables in the following pattern (2-4-6-8-2) It also contains five lines, and often, one word in the first line, two words in the second line, etc:

MORE THAN WORDS (traditional style)
I am
So much more than
The poetry you read.
Just once...look away and indulge
In me.

CLIMAX (modern style)
Bedsheets
Silky....smooth

PHIYAH PHLOW

Slipping...sliding....entangling
Submersing us deeper into
Warmth

THANK YOU (traditional style)
You love
My inner glow.
You always tell me so.
It's because you rescued me from
Darkness.

WILL YOU SHUT UP ALREADY
(traditional style)
I write
Both day and night.
Hoping to shush the voice
That continues to make me write
Day…night.

SIGH….. (modern style)
Dishes.
Piled up.
Crusting. Crumbing. Icky'ing.
I hear them screaming
"WASH ME!"

YUMMY (modern style)
Cooking.
Sweet smells.
Teasing. Taunting. Tantalizing.
Time to dig in!
Bon Appetit!

TWO PAIR (traditional style)
Your lips.
Plushy pillows.

PHIYAH PHLOW

Sweet and delectable.
Teasing. Licking. Sucking. Tasting.
Kiss…me…
Written: December 2, 2014
WHEN WILL IT STOP? NOBODY KNOWS
(traditional style)

Trayvon.
Sean Bell. Mike Brown.
Renisha. Tanesha.
Jordan. Eric. Akai. Tamir.
ENOUGH!

MR. OFFICER…WE REALLY DO MATTER
(traditional style)
Police.
Protect and serve?
To assist? To assume?
To harass? To beat? To murder?
DON'T SHOOT!

NOW THAT'S SEXY!
(modern style)
Sexy.
Tits. Ass.
Shaking. Bouncing. Everywhere-Flaunting.
Guess what's REALLY sexy….
My mind.

(traditional style)
Sexy.
What does it mean?
Big tits? Or a fat ass?
Neither one is sexier than
My heart.

PHIYAH PHLOW

GOOD MORNING (modern style)
Waking.
Bodies close.
Caressing. Cuddling. Neck-Nuzzling.
Spooning easily transitions into
"Forking."

COITUS ON A CORD

Ring
Ring....
Ring
Ring....

That sound....so sweet
In my left ear
Upon answering
It's your delicious voice I hear

Heart on steroids
Palpitation
Ready to drown
In this conversation

I realize we spoke
Just yesterday
But my panties still perspire
In anticipation of what we'll say

Our lingo is so loose
We care not about the time
4 hours giving head....
We always blow each other's minds

I suck on his....sentence structure
He grubs on my....correct grammar
Bustin' nuts over nouns and pronouns
Dangling participle hits hard like a sledgehammer

This really vexes me
Because the complexity
Of this "thang" that we share
Truly perplexes me

PHIYAH PHLOW

See even though we have yet
To dig in each other's sex
We always orgasm
At the close of each text

Drenched in sweat
Wondering how much longer it'll be
Before I can ride on his ocean
While he swims in me

These miles that separate us
Have become painfully absurd
So until we're finally able to touch
We just fuck each other's words

PHIYAH PHLOW

DEEP ROOTS

Seeds scattered upon the earth deep within the dirt
Water flows down to raise you up
You become stronger
Taller
Harder
Branches begin to spring forth from every part of you
Stronger
Taller
Harder
Sun smiles down upon you
Wind rips fiercely through your leaves
Do you see how I admire you
Your strength
Your over-whelming power over me
You and are now one
You are my mighty oak
My leaves
My branches
My bark
A tree

Originally Titled: JUST A TREE
Original Write: Freshman Year at USC – Columbia, November 1992
Slight Revision and Re-Title: June 10, 2014

PHIYAH PHLOW

DINNER IS SERVED

The more you say it to me
The more I believe it to be
And the more I believe it to be
The more with you I must agree

That
Thick
Girls
Taste
Better

So tell me what you have in mind
To feast upon tonight
This full-course meal of a body
Was specifically designed to whet a King's appetite

Let's start with some strawberry kisses on lips
That's dipped in a dark passion dream
Or would you prefer the taste of some fire red cherries
Soaked in love's whipped cream

Sugar-coated nipples perfectly perched
Upon each milk - chocolate mound
Scoop each double D into the warmth of your mouth
Cuz I just love how you make that slurping sound

Never the one to impale in some wimpy ass spinach or kale
You prefer to sink your teeth in some meat
Well my mid-section is made from steak, potatoes and Kool-aid
So come gorge yourself on each succulent treat

PHIYAH PHLOW

Damn...you STILL hungry? You greedy mutha-fudga!
Well how'd you like summa this shake to go with your fries?
Just make sure you pace yourself because you gotta save some room
For your dessert that awaits between my thighs

The prettiest of peaches drenched in such syrupy sweetness
I know you crave a big juicy bite
And with produce THIS delectable, plucked fresh off the vine
I don't blame you for wanting to grub all night

And since
Thick
Girls
Taste
Better
I must taste scrumptiously amazing
From red rice to fried chicken to macaroni and collards
And them Hot Now Krispy Kremes oozing with the glazing

Now you drooling and shit; eyes popping out ya head
Trying to see if you got enough room on your plate
To fit at least a couple more of these honey butter biscuits
Even though your greedy ass just ate

You've dubbed my body "Insatiable"
The voracity of your hunger is beyond real

PHIYAH PHLOW

Quarter Pounders with cheese just don't have the nutrients to please
You stay full and content off THIS Happy Meal

Mmmmm...I love how you look at me
Like you just can't wait to cut you a huge slice of this Heaven
Thank God we both have jobs to go to
Otherwise I'd stay spread out 24/7

Oh but don't you worry daddy, I'll never shut down the buffet
At least not until you've truly had all-you-can-eat
So feel free to roast me, skewer me, fuckin' kebab me
From the top of my head to the soles of my feet

Dinner is served so pull on up to the table
Grab your knife and your fork and dig in
And when you're done, gone sleep that shit off, cuz soon as you wake up
It'll be time to eat again...

PHIYAH PHLOW

FOREVER MEANS FOREVER... RIGHT?

She said she was ready
She better be
Most of her sista/friends
Were already 20 years in
Some were working on round 2
A few were already on 3 and 4
And here she was
40
One man-child drenched in a separate legacy
Attached to her hip
Yet SHE still bears her same name
Ain't that a damn shame
Mortgages and mothers-in-law
Cheeks filled with way too much sugar and
Choices between Disneyland and the backyard
For this year's family vacation
Dogs
Cats
Goldfish
Iguanas
All dreams of her "Forever"
Had somehow eluded her all these years

So OF COURSE when "Hmm...Maybe" came along
She jumped on "Possibility's" train
I mean hey
Why risk "Never" coming back around again
Right
But alas, he, "Perhaps," wasn't ready to be her "Forever"
And apparently no amount of

Praying or
Prodding or
Pressing or
Pouting or
Please baby, baby please
Prepared him for THIS day

THIS was supposed to be her walk into
"FINALLY"
Through her white picket fence
Into "I never gotta take out the trash myself again"
Into "I never gotta pump my own gas again"
Into "Thank you Jesus…now I won't grow old and die alone"
Into "Happily Ever After"
Into "FINALLY…I have someone who will love me…Forever"

Man
What the hell kinda sorry-ass fairy-tale is
THIS
"Forever" didn't whisk her away into the sunset
Like she'd "forever" envisioned
Oh no
Instead
She remains seated here
Alone
In her "Frantic Reality"
And as if punched in the gut
With the closed fist of "Clarity"
She comes to the frightful conclusion that

"Perhaps"
Here
Where she sits now
Alone

PHIYAH PHLOW

Is in fact
Her
"Forever"

FOUR LINE DROPS

FOR SALE
The last tenant moved out abruptly
Leaving cracks and holes in every spot
I told you it would take time to repair the damage
And you said, "Time is all that I got."

SQUEAKY CLEAN
I just took a shower
Everything's scrubbed all nice and clean
So now how bout you slide me in your mouth
And chew me like a stick of Dentyne??

TRAGIC
If I had a dime for all of the times
You made me feel special or treated me kind
Ever blew my mind or made me feel fine
I'd be a dime short every single time

AHHHHH
There's no greater feeling in the world
Absolutely none that could ever, EVER match
The joy of getting home, snatching off your bra
And enjoying a good "under boob" scratch

OH U EEN KNOW
Dem boi always talkin' bout
Een nuffin new unda da sun
But when e come to a Geechie Gurl
All Dem Boi Want One!
"Geechie Gurl: All Dem Boi Want One" used with permission from Erica Michelle Alcox, founder and CEO of Geechie Gurl, Inc

PHIYAH PHLOW

GOOD MORNING
Arms and legs remain intertwined
Remnants of love from the night before
We ignore the sun's rays pressing through the blinds
And disappear into us once more

SAY IT LOUD
Guns aim. Grey bullets scatter.
Bodies rain. Red blood splatters.
Mothers wail in pain. Little brown feet never again pitter-patter.
Say it loud with no shame...Black lives DO matter!

I'LL SEE YOU WHEN YOU GET BACK HOME
The words "DON'T SHOOT" on the back of his shirt; I guess they didn't see
Pleading didn't help; they STILL took my boy from me
His spirit haunts me daily; and I don't wanna be free
Never to kiss his face again....I just hug his memory

PHIYAH PHLOW

GIMME 5

I have 5 favors to ask of you
And I promise every one will
Bring you pleasure too

I'd like to SEE
You watching me
Willing me with your eyes
To set you free
From the mundane
Loves you used to know
And make the sky the limit
To how far this goes

I'd like to FEEL
You invade my space
As I welcome your breath
Upon my face
And eagerly await
Your fingertips
As you trace your desire
Across my lips

I'd like to TASTE "I want you"
In the depths of your tongue
You know you've got me
Mmmm yes I'm sprung
Our spirits have connected
Two souls in tune
The stars have aligned
And as we orbit the moon

I'd like to HEAR
You scream my name
And I don't care which one you call me

PHIYAH PHLOW

Whether Tiffany or Jayne
Just scream it into the night
And make it sound so true
That even the owls
Won't need to question "WHO"

Do you SMELL that? Recognize that scent?
That's the essence of two lovers
Wrapped in sugary sweat
Longing for the darkness to trade places with the sun
I appreciate the 5 favors
Guess now I owe you 1

PHIYAH PHLOW

GIVE ME THAT BACK!

Oh yessss
What might this be
This smooth chocolate landscape
Spread before me

Making me shudder
Taking my breath
Causing me to gasp
With the little I have left

Teasing me…taunting me
From across the floor
Whispering my name
Making me want you more

Perfectly broad
Stretched from East to West
I love ALL your body parts
But this one here, is the BEST

Its lines so defined
As I watch you work out
Its valleys and peaks so unique
Got me giddy for a "work out"

So rock solid in its strength
It shows no fear of manual labor
The anticipation of its nakedness
Trips my mind to thoughts of naughty behaviors

The weights of EVERY world
Leave it so battered and bruised
But YOURS is still the most
Beautiful skin I've ever perused

PHIYAH PHLOW

Hard as a rock
Yet somehow soft as a baby's hide
Family roots singe so deep
It exudes honor and pride

And as I happily towel off
The day's droplets of sweat
I massage it and kiss it
And pray away its debts

I just can't help but smile
Because I've been waiting for what's next
As you lay my body down
My fingers dance across those pecs

Knowing without a doubt
That there will probably never be
Any body part as enticingly beautiful
As a man's back is to me

PHIYAH PHLOW

HAPPY MISERY

I've stunned her into silence
I feel her watching me walk away
She just can't believe
The news she's received
She has no words to say

It was never my intent to hurt her
Where she stands now, I've stood many times before
The lies and deceit
Pain stuck on repeat
Heartbreak that cuts down to the core

She calls me a bitch and a home wrecker
She asks me how I didn't know
I tell her he never ONCE mentioned her name
But she still sees ME as the blame
To her, I'm nothing but a ho

He's playing us BOTH for fools
He's putting us BOTH through hell
And the tears we BOTH weep
Prove we're BOTH in too deep
And in a few months, my belly will start to swell

But the one thing we BOTH can agree on
Is that HE needs to make a decision TODAY
Whether it's her or it's me
We can BOTH plainly see
That NEITHER of us is strong enough to walk away

We BOTH have too much to lose
So if he's refuses to choose
This "happy misery" is where we'll BOTH stay

PHIYAH PHLOW

HE IS MY "G" SPOT

This
Beautiful
Black
Brother
Divinely dipped in ethereal excellence
Makes mountains move when it comes to
Me
He calls me his
Quintessential queen

His
Thick-up Thug

His
Gorgeous Gangsta

His
Inspirational ink that "Phlows" passion through his pen
He no longer craves
Fhyisical food
Because
The sustenance of my soul's sugary sweetness
Purposefully penetrates him with all the
nourishment he needs to aNnihilate nations
And I
Graciously grant him all my glorious givings
Because
He is my
Kingdom's keeper

My
Perfect prophesy

PHIYAH PHLOW

My
Rock-hard Rameses

My
Metaphysical movement

He's the
Rhythmical reason behind every lusciously, lustfully,
love-filled lyric
He has
Feloniously fucked me twenty times since Tuesday
Using
Nothing More
Than
Nouns and Metaphors
We are
Each other's
Secret soliloquy
Hushed hearts harbored among the breeze
Such a torridly tantalizing treat
Cunningly candid conversations make our voracious
verbal exchanges complete

This juicy juxtaposition
Has us both weak....wantonly wishin'
For opulent overdoses of

This
Magical mojo

This
Diabolical dripping

This
Exemplary ecstasy

PHIYAH PHLOW

This
Alluringly affable affair

This
Beautiful
Black
Brother
Who moves massive mountains
For I
His Quintessential queen
Really GETS me
So he can get IT
Anytime....

PHIYAH PHLOW

I QUIT YOU

We all have tribulations
We all have trials
We all got bills that stretch
For miles and miles

Most of us hate our jobs
Some of us hate the cars we drive
But damn can you at least ACT like
You happy to be alive

Every single time I see you
You got your "screw face" on
Like every thing that happens
In your life is all wrong

You enter a room
And every living thing dies
Cuz every word outta your mouth
Is a "woe is me" or a "sigh"

May I please ask you why
Are you so fuckin dry
You constantly talk yourself out
Of your piece of the pie

And the longer I hung around you
The more I did the same
Always negative
Always pissy
Looking for someone else to blame

For all the unhappy things
That were happening in my life
Why can't I pay my bills

PHIYAH PHLOW

Why didn't he make me his wife

Why I ain't go no money
Why my son acting a fool
Why my house ain't fly
Why my car ain't cool

Why my backyard ain't got a pool
Why does my life my suck
Why can't I lay in the middle of the street
And get hit by a bread truck

And then I finally realized
That the problems were all mine
Stop the negative talk
And maybe my shit will be fine

But to make this thing work
And be able to push through
I have to keep myself separated
From people like you

And that includes you
Even though you still my gurl
I just ain't got time for
All that negative bullshit in my world

So perhaps I'll holla once you get ya mind right
But until then…I guess you'll be a'ight

PHIYAH PHLOW

I THOUGHT YOU WERE DEAD

I didn't think you'd ever return
Not even sure why you're here
Bombarding my mind
Clouding my thoughts
Wanting me to shed tears again
Making me return to my 12 year old self
Beating myself down

Knowing I caused "this" to happen
"You're so stupid!"
"Why'd you even open the door dummy?"
"You shouldn't have let him hug you!"
"You asked for that!"

You stole my voice
I couldn't tell my mother
Or even my aunt....who I ALWAYS told
EVERYTHING to
My grandmother had just died
They were already sad
You told me if I told them
I'd make them sadder

What I feel in my heart
Has a horrible habit of taking up residence
On my face

My mouth said "Fine" when mommy asked how I was
My face said....
"Why?? Can you tell he was here?"
"Do you smell his breath on me? He kissed my neck..."

PHIYAH PHLOW

"Do my shorts still show remnants of his greasy hand print? He squeezed my bottom..."

You said my grandmother was a wonderful woman
As you kissed my neck
And squeezed my bottom
And at that moment
I hated my body

I hated my over developed breasts
I hated my over developed bottom
I hated this 21 year old's body
Trying to masquerade as a 12 year old's

My body confused you
Made you take unjust advantage of your
"Friend of the Family" status
And when my mother told me years later that you had passed away
A shrug and an "oh yeah?" was my only reply

Little did she know
You died years ago
At least to me anyway
See, the day I opened the door for you
The same day you hugged me too hard
Which is the same day you hugged me too long
Also the same day you kissed my neck
And squeezed my bottom
All while telling me my grandmother was a wonderful woman

I killed you
And buried you
And banished you straight to hell
You've died 1000 deaths over the years

PHIYAH PHLOW

Yet here you are....alive and well

Well no Mr. So-and-So
You may have molested my innocence yesterday
But I will NOT allow you to continue to molest my spirit today

I didn't think you'd ever return
Not even sure why you're here
But the 41 year old me
Just presented my 12 year old self
With the bestest gift she could ever ask for.....

Her voice

PHIYAH PHLOW

I WRITE BECAUSE…

I write because nobody listens
I spill my ink over pipe dreams and wishes
Praying for strength as my tears start to fall
Lord help me reach the masses or no one at all
Hand them my heart with a bow wrapped around it
Used to not have a voice but thanks to Poetry, I found it
I refuse to be silenced, I got TOO much shit to say
No longer caring who's listening cuz I'mma spit anyway
And with my fist clenching my pen, I raise it high in the air
Whatchu wanna hear today folks?
Truth or dare?

I write because nobody listens
And because God didn't allow it to kill my vision
Words slice through my heart like a lyrical incision
Ink fires like bullets hitting the page like ammunition
Bringing every thought that I've wrought to fruition
Releasing this poetic beast is my soul's only mission
Spittin' whatever the hell I feel, never seeking permission
Each write is an orgasm, a well-versed emission
Tongue-lashing every ear with diabolical precision
Now look what you miss when you don't pay attention…

PHIYAH PHLOW

JUST SAY THANK YOU AND SHUT UP

I can't speak yet about tomorrow
But as for today, I's feelin fine
I woke up singing high notes
With nothing but positives on my mind
Planted my feet upon my floor
And stretched my hands to the ceiling in praise
And bellowed a resounding "THANK YOU FATHER
Cuz this here body You didn't even have to raise
But simply cuz You saw fit to do so
My day is already blessed
Which is why the foot I choose to put forward
Will represent my very best"
So I get washed up and brush my teeth
I got my fro stacked high to the sky
And while I'm not rockin' Versace or Gucci
I'm STILL looking stone-cold fly
My jeans are hugging my hips just right
And my top has the boobies showing just enough
I smile at my reflection and say
"Girl you are HAWT"
And my reflection giggles and says
"Oh STAWP!"
I bounce out the door with a spring in my step
Not concerned about the troubles I may face today
"For in you I have not instilled the spirit of fear"
That's in Your Word, and I believe what You say
So whatever it is I may be going through
Or whatever it is I may lack
I ain't e'en much guh wor' bout um
Cuz Gawd, I dun know You got my back

PHIYAH PHLOW

KEEP CALM AND JUST FAKE IT TIL YOU MAKE IT

OR TIL ENOUGH IS FINALLY ENOUGH; BUT YOU ALREADY KNOW GOOD AND DAMN WELL FOLKS WILL BE DRINKING ICE WATER IN HELL BEFORE YOU LEAVE SO JUST REFER BACK TO THE FIRST 10 WORDS IN THIS TITLE AND HAVE A NICE DAY

Don't cry Tiff
Don't cry Tiff
Tiff please don't cry
DO NOT CRY!
Stay "asleep"
Don't even acknowledge his presence
Hopefully he'll just take his ass on to sleep

Just ignore the funk of fried pork chops and Japanese Cherry Blossom so disrespectfully punching you in the nostrils right now

Resist the urge to scoot so close to the edge of the bed that you're precisely 2.5 seconds from kissing the carpet because you don't want to risk his lips, no doubt still smeared with her sweetness like Chap Stick, to graze your neck

Allow his fingers to continue rubbing your pudge, even though you know for a fact that those same fingers just professed their love for her chocolaty smooth thickness

Please keep your face turned to the window
Do NOT turn around

PHIYAH PHLOW

Do not stare pitifully….yearningly…..in his face
Do NOT give this mutha-fucka the satisfaction of taking ownership of even ONE tear potentially caressing your cheek
Do not bless his ass with even one whimpered "Why?"

Do NOT fix your mouth to beg him
Yet again
To love you
JUST you
AND ONLY YOU GOT'DAMMIT!
Not her
Or her
Her either
OH! And that skanky bitch whose roach-invested house he JUST left??
MOST DEFINITELY NOT HER!

Yes…good girl
Just lay still
Don't even breathe

You already know that this pain you're feeling is so much worse at night
Because the darkness has yet to greet you both in the house at the same time
But it's all good
The sun is right around the corner from the moon
And you'll have yet
ONE MORE DAY
To prove yourself
Worthy
Of finally winning
His heart

PHIYAH PHLOW

KEEPS ON SLIPPIN'

I need more of you.
I hate your elusiveness.
Please stop teasing me.

You're never enough.
Searching but never finding
Extra grains of you.

Every missed second...
Every single lost hour....
I placed blame on you.

But yet you blamed me.
Said if I budget better
You'll always be here.

Well where are you now?
I'm here crying out for you
But you don't respond.

How does that song go?
"Time keeps on slippin'....slippin'..."
I feel you slippin'....

Is that the right time?
It's not earlier than that?
Where DID the time go?

I thought we had time....
Thought you'd always wait for me....
Damn....guess I was wrong..

PHIYAH PHLOW

LET'S EAT

Candles lit
Incense burning
Coochie jumping
Body's yearning
Wine is chilling
Mood is set
Come and get it
I'm so wet
Eyes are closed
Legs are open
Heart is racing
Ready, hopin
French kiss the lips
Below my face
Little lower
Have a taste
Ain't she yummy
Honey sweet
Lick some more
Breathe….repeat
Grab my ass
Lift me higher
Stoke these embers
Fan this fire
My eyes are crossing
I grab your head
You got me flailing
All over this bed
My back is arched
My toes broke-bent
I have no idea
Where my "lady-like" went
This feels so good
I can't control my screams

PHIYAH PHLOW

You're trying to lick me dry
Or so it seems
My stomach's in knots
My thighs are quivering
Hips gyrating
Whole body shivering
I fall back on the pillows
Waterfalls released
I say, "Thank you for dining sir,
Hope you enjoyed your feast"
You say, "Nothing beats home-cooking
From the South"
I say, "Glad you liked it
Now wipe your mouth"

PHIYAH PHLOW

LIE LIKE YOU MEAN IT

Tell me I'm beautiful
Tell me I'm sexy
Tell me I'm everything you want
Everything you need
Everything you crave
Tonight
Tell me you can't breathe without me
Tell me your life has no meaning without me
Tell me you've missed me
Tell me you've fantasized only of me
Tell me how sleep has become a faint breeze that escapes you
Because I'm no longer there for you to inhale my intoxicating scent
Tell me I'm yours
Tell me you're mine
Just for tonight
Don't tell me you want to fuck me
Tell me you want to make love to me
Because that is what lovers do when they're truly
In love
Tell me you want to transform my bedroom into a studio
And wrap my body inside of a beautiful ballad
Composed of calories and crescendos bursting forth from my candid cries
Tell me this is not a dream
Tell me this is real
Tell me this is what you truly feel
Tell me you never want to leave
Tell me you mean it
Wrap me in your arms
And moan luscious lullabies in my ear

PHIYAH PHLOW

Until I, at last, drift off into my soul's sweetest slumber
And when I awake in the morning
Please be gone
Because if I arise to the prickling of your breath on my skin
I'll be inclined to believe
That every word you whispered to me the night before
Was true

LOOK AWAY

I wonder if you're able to look through me
Deep into my soul and really see
How fake I truly am

All you see is my forever smile
Not realizing that for quite a while
I've been forever dying inside

The constant jokes I crack...all for a laugh
Would probably make you cry if you only knew the half
Sometimes I feel my life ain't worth a damn

Please....don't stare at me for too long
I don't want you to figure out what's really wrong
I still have secrets I'd like to continue to hide

Don't you worry about me
My reflection is all you need to see
Because right now....all I have left IS my pride

PHIYAH PHLOW

LOVE MY ASS

Yes love is patient
And love is kind
But negro your love had me on the verge
Of losing my mind
Forgetting who I was
By taking on YOUR life
Praying hard for the day
That you'd me make your wife
Showing you my skills
In the bedroom and the kitchen
Trying to make you understand
It's ME your life's missing
Ignoring my family's warnings
And pushing my friends to the side
Continuing to breathe life into you
Regardless of the times I died
Or the times I've cried
Over your bullshit and lies
But now I reclaim my soul
While realizing there's plenty other guys
Out here who'll respect me
Way more than you ever have
"But baby I love you!!"
Sheeiiit please don't make me laugh
Now get the hell from my door
Before I call the police
And have you arrested
For disturbing my peace..

PHIYAH PHLOW

METHAPHORE WHORE

Why am I so nervous?
Palms sweaty like first dates
Should I dive in face first?
Or swim to safety like first mates?

Man I can't even think straight
My mind is blown
Dy-no-mite
JJ's bravado escapes me though
And I think that perhaps I should call it a night

Try this challenge another day
Maybe then I'll have something to say
But I got nothing but blank stares
For these blank sheets
And my words are D.O.A.
Dead On Arrival
Unable to resuscitate

And just like trying to make a dolla outta 15 cents
This shit right here ain't maiking no sense

What the hell did I agree to this challenge for?
I'm a Metaphorical Virgin
Trying to front like she's a whore
These stars are rolling deep tonight
So lemme go on and kick this wish:
Please let me drop some metaphors
At least 2, maybe more
So I can spit some ill shit like this:

AHEM…

PHIYAH PHLOW

Yeah dem birds may touch the sky
But they still ain't fly as me
And even wit' the needle in ya arm
You'll still never soar high as me
Gimme a D
Gimme an O
Gimme a P
Gimme an E
You got all the letters in the alphabet
And you STILL ain't DOPE as me
You just can NOT figga me out
Like Pi equals what??
But this MC is far from square
Now go try to figga THAT out
Awww yeah I'm on a roll
And ain't no butter involved
Your head is spinning outta control
Like them doors that revolve
Yeah I'm feeling myself
And I got every right to
Because just like everything else
I do that better than you too
Yeah I know that was harsh
But hey, the truth is the truth
My name might not be Bishop
But I still got dat "Juice"

Sigh…man if I was clever like THAT
I'd ALWAYS rip crazy shit like that
But since I don't know how to bring the
Metaphorical Pain
I'll just metaphorically stay in my own damn lane

PHIYAH PHLOW

MY BAD Y'ALL

To all the guys I've loved before
I owe every last one of you
An apology
And I mean that sincerely
From the very bottom of the same heart
That you each ripped to shreds
See even though it was YOU
Who cheated on ME
And YOU who always made ME cry
And YOU who continued to spoon feed ME
Little appetizers of your love
Because you very quickly discovered that I was a "cheap date"
And would never see myself worthy of demanding
The full course meal of your commitment and respect
I understand now
That it is I who inevitably forced your hand
I erroneously placed the entire burden
Of MY happiness
On YOUR shoulders
I expected YOU
To be ALL of the things
That my father never was to me
I expected YOU
To lose yourself in ME
Just as I'd disappeared into you
I expected YOU
To forget you had a life
Before ME
Just as I'd suddenly developed
A severe case of amnesia for you
When you moved, I moved
Just like that

PHIYAH PHLOW

And I expected you to do the same
I expected YOU
To be MY savior
I expected each one of YOU
To be the one to unpack ALL of the baggage
That I was still carrying
From each of my previous "road trips"
I expected YOU to be
Perfect
And anything less was unacceptable
And no ONE person
Deserves THAT kind of pressure
Placed upon them
And for all of that
I am deeply sorry
By NO means am I condoning or accepting
Any hurtful thing that any of you ever did to me
But I CAN accept the fact that because my lifelong insecurities
Kept ME from loving ME properly
None of YOU could love me properly
So to all the guys I've loved before
Thank you for indirectly teaching me
The TRUE meaning of love
By showing me that I can't expect
ANY man to give me the
Love, acceptance and respect that I crave
If I haven't even given it to myself

PHIYAH PHLOW

NO DOZE

(Spoken in the Voice of a Man on His Last Legs)

I really don't want to go to sleep.
You see, going to sleep TONIGHT
Means that TOMORROW is inevitable.

Another tomorrow I don't think I have the strength to survive.

Another tomorrow filled with job opportunities,
That turn into maybe's,
That usually end with cemented doors slammed in my face.

Another tomorrow dreading the walk to the mailbox because
I already know that million dollar check still ain't in there.

Another tomorrow dodging the "unknown caller."

She doesn't say it…
But she doesn't need to.
Her eyes,
And this invisible line in our bed,
Says it all…

She's sick of this shit.

And I don't blame her.
I have no doubt in my mind that she loves me.
I have no doubt in my mind that she will be my "ride or die"
Til the end of time.

PHIYAH PHLOW

But time is running out on my sanity Lord!
My weeping has endured for FAR too many tonights.
And I seriously think that if my joy doesn't come tomorrow,
Sleep and I will probably never be friends again..

PHIYAH PHLOW

ODE TO THE D

GOT'DAMN
Your dick
That Magic Stick
9 beautiful inches
And perfectly thick
I love it when you grip
That Powerful Prick
And rub the tip on my clit
Til it's all moist and slick
And then oh so quick….ly you glide in
And now you're bump….in and you're grind…..in
And you're hitting and splitting every single crevice
As you're dipping and ripping through every orifice
You're in me so deep, I feel you in the back of my throat
Tickling my esophagus, damn near making me choke
And then you back my ass up against the wall
Lifting me and gripping me so that I don't fall
You stretch my thighs from west to east
And start pounding this pussy like a savage beast
I'm scratching your back and shrieking your name
Your dick is going ever deeper, I think it's tapping my brain
You got me spread so wide I think my body's bout to break
I don't know how much more of this dick I can take
In and out and out and in
I understand now why fornication is a sin
Dick THIS fucking good is truly an adDICKtion
And if I couldn't get this on the regular, it'd be a contraDICKtion
Mmmmmmm…...oooowwwww this hurts so good

PHIYAH PHLOW

My body's growing limp from your Wonderful Wood
Your Jungle Johnson, your Super Sperm
Your Big Baller, your Wicked Worm
And with each and every thrust, my walls come down
My pussy was once lost but now she's found
The more I buck, the more you fuck
The more you slide, the more I ride
The more I scratch and claw and scream
The deeper your spoon scoops out my cream
And right when it seems that it just can't get no better
One final plunge completely changes my weather
My drought is now over, my dryness washed out
Now THAT'S what the fuck I'm talkin bout
GOT'DAMN
Your Dick
Your GOT'DAMN Dick
That Magic Stick
What a Powerful Prick
And I love it…..oops I mean YOU….yeah I love you

PHIYAH PHLOW

OFFICIALLY OFF THE MARKET

The last tenant moved out in the wee hours of the morning
Politely backed the U-Haul up to the side door and proceeded to pack up half of the "forever" we'd planned together
Said he'd outgrown the cramped quarters and needed more space to move around
I tried to negotiate a new contract with him
Told him I'd get rid of some of my shoes so he'd have more closet space
Told him I'd stop hogging all the sheets at night
Told him I'd be so quiet he'd forget I was even in the house
Just please....please.....please baby
With a cherry on top
Please....don't go

But apparently he'd been searching for a new place to lay his head for awhile
Because he'd already paid his deposit and his new "landlord" was patiently awaiting his arrival
Please baby....with a cherry on top....don't go
He said "sorry Love..."
And shut the door behind him

FOR SALE:
One heart
Bruised and battered
Torn and tattered
Former tenant caused major damage
Left walls covered in blood spatter
Much work needs to be done
And I'm not sure how long it'll take to repair
But it's a beautiful fixer-upper

PHIYAH PHLOW

Long as you got some time to spare

And so there it sat
Cobwebs beginning to form in every crevice and corner
As I patiently awaited new love's arrival
While secretly still hoping for old love's return
Oh a few prospects breezed through from time-to-time
But they either lacked the patience required to turn this old rundown shack into a beautiful new mansion
Or I just didn't trust them enough to maintain the necessary upkeep
I began to lose all hope that these 4 walls would ever again know how it feels to be filled with love
And so, in the wee hours of the morning,
I dejectedly decided to take down my....

"Excuse me Miss
I hope this space is still available.
I should've come through months ago, but whenever I saw someone else checking it out, I'd lose hope...believing I'd missed my chance.
But seeing that it's still empty,
I'd love to come inside and take a look around..."

Past experiences had me primed to say no...
Yet something told me that this time...it would be different
Anxiety took over as he stepped inside
And as he slowly, yet calmly, perused the severe wear and tear,
Fear began to speak loudly in my ear...

Too much damage has been done

PHIYAH PHLOW

He's going to think it's too bruised and battered
Too torn and tattered
He's going to notice that the walls require too much
paint to cover up all the blood spatter

I quietly said,
"Much work needs to be done
And I'm not sure how long it'll take to repair;
But it's a beautiful fixer-upper
Long as you got some time to spare."

He took one last look around,
Then he looked at me,
Smiled,
And asked....
"So when can I move in?"

PHIYAH PHLOW

OPEN LETTER FROM THE EX-MAN TO THE NEXT MAN

All the digging in your pockets
All the rifling through your things
All the side-eye looks she gives you
Every time your phone rings

All the questions and accusations
All the snooping and the prying
All the ranting and the raving
And the attitudes and crying

Every time you walk out the door
And she's hurling profanities at your back
Don't be mad at her
Blame me for all of that

When I met her she exuded confidence
But thanks to me, it's now non-existent
Oh she tried to walk away from me numerous times
But my dick was far too persistent

The few times she was actually strong enough to leave
The urgency in my words always drew her back in
"Yes baby, I really DO love you with ALL of my heart
And I promise I'll NEVER cheat on you again"

And every time I said it, I really did mean it
And I'd even behave myself for a little while
But all it took was the curve of another woman's ass

PHIYAH PHLOW

Or the seduction behind another woman's smile

I'd make her put all her trust back in me
Only for us to revisit the same ol scene
She was aggressively begging me to be her King
But in her, I just didn't see my Queen

Now her issues are flashing like a neon sign
And I gave a name to every single one
The main 3 being "Please Marry Me,"
"Please Take Care of Me" and "Please be a Daddy to My Son"

Man, I played off all that shit
Told her EVERYTHING she needed to hear
To make her believe I was her proverbial "knight in shining armor"
And that I'd one day whisk her away from here

But instead I just bided my time
Until I was ready to move along
To the next woman who firmly has my heart on lock
The same heart your girl wanted all along

And so now that I've broken her spirit
She's severely emotionally weak
And she's looking at you to give her
All of the happiness that she seeks

I already know she be on that bullshit
And it's getting more fucked up by the day
And she'll probably never trust you or your words
No matter what you say

So just walk softly, keep shit quiet

PHIYAH PHLOW

Try not to give her a reason to bitch
And if one day you finally get tired of all that shit
My lady has a sister I can hook you up with

POETRY IS…

Poetry is…

What it's always been
My late-night lover
My all-day friend
My hand-holder when I feel alone
On this massive earth
The seed I've nursed since birth
Poetry showed me my worth
They're the words that God
Has chosen me to release
In the midst of raging storms
Poetry is my peace

It turns me on
It turns me out
It transitioned my diminutive voice
Into a shout
It makes me believe
I'm able to receive
It allows me to laugh
It allows me to grieve
It's my 100 watt bulb
In the darkest of night
It gives me the strength
To continue my fight
These sheets become my boxing ring
This pen…my gloves
And no matter how severe the blood "Phlows"
It's STILL love

Poetry is you
Poetry is me
Poetry is us

PHIYAH PHLOW

Poetry is we
Poetry is our truth
And it will always be free
Poetry is my permission
To be…

POETRY SAID I COULD

You stepped to me at time when my voice
Was non-existent
Unsure of the woman I was becoming
Afraid to trouble the waters
Because of the impending storms ahead
No need to speak
The people I wanted to hear me
Weren't listening anyway

But you got me blossoming
Uprooting my words like flowers from fresh soil
Never judging what I say
Or how I choose to say it
You told me I have the right to speak
Whether it be from my heart
Or from the very pits of my soul
You told me I have the right to speak

Whether it be about love's blissful beginnings
Or the putrid stench of its bitter demise
From joy to pain
From sunshine to rain
From happy to sad
From good to bad
From perfectly pissed to disgustingly dissed
From dawn's early light to my first and last kiss

One line
Two lines
Three lines
Four
You gave me back to me
Plus so much more
My confidence

PHIYAH PHLOW

My strength
My peace
My heart
My voice

This voice that has the audacity to believe that it
Shouldn't be silenced
After all
It was YOU who told me I have the right to speak
So out of ANY pen
Onto ANY page
Into ANY mic
Standing firmly on ANY stage

Speak?   Sheeeiiit….you asked for it! ;-)

PHIYAH PHLOW

QUALITY TIME

I cherish moments like these.
They come so few and far in between now.
You know how it is sometimes…
We start off talking every day;
Life takes over;
And before you know it,
Months have gone by since I was last in
Your presence.

But today…
It's time you and I reconnect with each other.
I need You to speak to me.
I need You to speak IN to me.

Your Words ebb through my spirit like the tide,
forever washing away any doubt that I've ever had
about your true feelings for me.

No matter how deep my pain you always manage
to wrap my heart tenderly in Your palms and
massage each pain away, as though your fingers
are intricately caressing every piano keyed
transgression.

When the troubles of this world become far too
much
for me to bear alone, You open Your arms to me
and I
boldly run into them every time,
unashamed and unconcerned about
who may be watching or what they may be saying.

You are my rock.
You are my strength.

PHIYAH PHLOW

You are my footprints in the sand.
You are my Do-Re-Mi-Fa-So-La-Ti-Do…

Oh!
How marvelous you are to me!

With You I am so free…

So if it's ok with You,
can we
please pretend like we never lost contact
and pick up where we left off?

Because

As I'm sure You already know…

We have A LOT of catching up to do...

PHIYAH PHLOW

REEEEWIIIIIIND

THEY say everything happens for a reason
And that some situations are only for a season
Is this true? Or are THEY just appeasin'?

See, if I had done ANYTHING differently
I wonder would I still be
The same ol' Tiffany?

From dropping outta college
Way back in 90-fo'
To chasing behind every mutha-fucka
I ain't even wit' no mo'

From trying so hard to fit in
That I sometimes missed standing out
To every opportunity I allowed to escape my grasp
Because my faith wasn't strong as my doubt

From spreading my legs way more
Than I've ever lifted my hands
To never questioning those things
I just couldn't understand

From being arrested
To double homelessness
From "baby daddy" drama
To sinking deeper in distress

Every single trial
I've ever been through
I swore I'd die in my sorrow
But God already knew

The scars have disappeared
And I no longer feel the burns
Because my life is simply a miniseries
Of lessons I have learned

Where I am right now
Is where I'm supposed to be
Yes I'm still in the struggle
But God's grace and mercy keeps my mind free

So yes in most circumstances
A "do-over" would sho nuff be swell
But for now, I'll just leave things the way that they are
That way, I've always got a story to tell

REMOVED

How dare you expose me
I wasn't ready
I didn't ask for any of this
I didn't ask for any of….you
I was perfectly fine (for the most part)
To remain hidden in my hurt
Pressed down in my pain
Deadlocked in my disappointment
It felt…dare I admit…safe
No chance of getting caught up
No chance of being let down
No way of tripping and falling
Face first
Into love's disrespectful grasp
I was perfectly fine (for the most part)
Being alone
And then here you came
And proved me a liar
Got me realizing that (for the most part)
I wasn't fine at all
Got me realizing precisely what I was missing along
This…this-ness
This…you-ness
And now I'm begging you to please
Release me from this rain
Purge me from this pain
Deliver me from my despair
Walls crumbled
Heart opened
Mask shattered
I have tripped
And fallen
Face first

PHIYAH PHLOW

Into love's all forgiving arms
The difference?
This time
I think I'm ready...

SAVE ME

(A Villanelle Poem)

I need to get up....but it's easier to stay asleep
So much on my mind....don't wanna think today
I'm far from depressed....but I'm drowning in the deep

Harder and faster....tears threaten to creep
"Darkness, please swallow the sun," I pray
I need to get up....but it's easier to stay asleep

Into my bones pain and sorrow do seep
Wrapped in my covers is where I'd much rather stay
I'm far from depressed....but I'm drowning in the deep

Quiet...please consume me...don't utter ne'er a peep
Choking on my words...I've nothing to say
I need to get up....but it's easier to stay asleep

No longer feeling strong...my soul begins to weep
A million pennies for a mere paltry of peace I would pay
I'm far from depressed....but I'm drowning in the deep

Clutching my final fragment of faith, I leap
Finally releasing my worries and allowing Him to have His way
I need to get up...I will not surrender to sleep
I'm far from depressed...no longer drowning in the deep..

PHIYAH PHLOW

SAY MY NAME!

T ook me a little minute but
I 've come to realize that I am
F iyah personified!
F ound my voice
A nd now I simply won't be quieted down!
N ever again will I be placed in ANYBODY'S box!
Y es I AM a force to be reckoned with!

T-I-F-F-A-N-Y

PHIYAH PHLOW

SHE LOVES ME

"She" wants "Me" to look at her
Without scrutinizing every single flaw
Without bashing every single dent in her skin
Without criticizing every single scar
See "she" thinks she is beautiful
And she wants "me" to see that too
But "she" is only a reflection of "me"
She has no idea what I've been through
Teased mercilessly all through school
Y'all know how kids are, bluntly mean and cruel
Limited creative insults, but never underestimate
the sting
"WIT' YA FAT SELF" tacked at the end of simple
attacks can bring
Always picked last for teams
"Man! Her fat self gon' make us lose!" they'd say
So I'd go all the way to the back of the line and
begin to pray
"Before it's my turn Lord, please let the bell ring
That way everybody's happy because I won't have
to do anything"
It's bad enough all the cute boys would look past
me
To all the pretty "red" or skinnier girls sitting right
behind me
When my mother lost her job, she could no longer
afford
To at least buy me all the cute clothes and shoes
From Sears and Montgomery Ward
So now not only am I fat, my gear is less than fly
Many of my weekends were spent at home
Where I'd eat and cry, and bitterly ask God,
"Why?!"

PHIYAH PHLOW

Why wasn't I born lighter? Why couldn't I be skinny?
I see beauty all AROUND me, but not necessarily IN me"
Low self-esteem began to bury my soul
It consumed my spirit and swallowed me whole
"Wuppin pa nub en all da wong places"
Kept me skinnin' and grinnin' in all the wrong faces
They said I was sexy just so they could sex me
Always hoping that THIS time, I'd be able to look back at THAT moment and say
"THIS is the one that never left me"
But as each one walked, they'd carry a piece of me along
Til my body grew weaker and my spirit was gone
"She" wants "Me" to tell her that I love her
But how can I say to this to her when I've never felt that for her
"She" made "Me" miserable because she chose not to be
What "My" convoluted perception of beauty came to be
I just wish "She" would go away and leave "Me" the hell alone
Because it's HER damn fault that I now sit here alone
With nobody to tell me how beautiful I am
How sexy I am
How intelligent I am
How worthy I am
How awesome I am
What a great mom I am
What a wonderful person I am
How deserving I am
Of love

PHIYAH PHLOW

And then "She" caresses "her" skin and wipes away her tears
And whispers so softly and lovingly in her ear
So quietly she speaks, yet the words rip the atmosphere
You are beautiful
You are sexy
You are intelligent
You are worthy
You are awesome
You are a great mom
You are a wonderful person
You are so deserving
Of love
And that's why I'll always love you
Do you believe "Me" when I say these things to you?"
And "She" smiles through her tears and says, "Yes, as a matter of fact, I do"

PHIYAH PHLOW

SHOW AND PROVE

It's been such a long time
How could I have left you
Without a PHIYAH PHLOW
To step to
Think of how many weak rhymes
Ya slept through
Camouflaged as the truth
Yet somehow they crept through

I know what you want
So I'mma give ya what ya need
This pen stabs deep in my chest
So you can watch my soul bleed

I don't   be playin' with these words
I make sure I be slayin' these words
I don't flock to every feather
So I came in flippin' these birds

You want Tiffany or Jayne?
They're both one in the same
See Tiffany spills the ink
While JPHLOW spits the pain

This ain't a game to me
I stay regurgitating on mics
I do this shit cuz I love it
While most folks feenin' for "likes"

I've rocked stages from Charlotte
To the A and in between
I rip pages, leaving scarlet letters
Behind at every scene

PHIYAH PHLOW

Did you catch that word play?
Or did it leave you CONfused?
See I'm a PRO at this every day
None of this PHLAYVA goes unused

I think I'm done speaking my peace
I brought the PHLOW heavy in this piece
See it's one thing to proclaim you're the greatest
And something else entirely to prove you're a beast

So hear me when I say this what the PHUCK I do
And I'mma do this til my last breath expends
Now this has been fun but please excuse me
I'm about to go "Play" some "Words" with my "Friends"

Written: March 10, 2015
First stanza written in the style of Eric B and Rakim's "I Know You Got Soul"

PHIYAH PHLOW

SOCIAL PROMOTION

"My kid is a SUPER STAR at Smart Kids Academy!"
"My kid EXCELS at the School of Excellence!"
"My kid makes ALL A's and B's at the School of Nothing But A's and B's!"

I see the bumper stickers.
I see the Facebook posts.
I see the pictures of smiling parents at awards ceremonies.
Holding up certificate after medal after trophy.
Praising their children for making
The Principal's Honor Roll,
The A/B Honor Roll,
Hell, even the Most Improved in Basket Weaving.
I see their kids making the All-County Band,
Achieving Violin First Chair in orchestra,
Playing basketball,
Football,
Volleyball,
Bocci Ball. (what the hell IS Bocci Ball anyway?)
Their children go to school everyday
And make their parents swell their chests with pride.
And then there's me….
Whose shoulders constantly slump in aggravated despair.
Because my son doesn't claim any of those categories.
He doesn't do his work,
He goes to sleep.
He doesn't participate in extra-curricular activities,
Unless of course being the class clown is now considered a sport.

PHIYAH PHLOW

He doesn't pay attention.
He doesn't listen.
He doesn't try harder than absolutely necessary.
He just….doesn't.
And I feel like a failure.
Because isn't it MY job to insure that my child
Passes the 9th grade?
And because he isn't passing,
Isn't it my fault?
I don't know what else to do.
He has the potential and the muscle to move mountains.
So why isn't he walking on through them?
How many more programs can I put him in?
How many more conversations can I have with him?
How many more meetings can I call at his school?
How many more extra credit assignments can I request?
How many more mentors and deacons and brother/friends can I have get in his face?
How much more yelling,
And screaming,
And punishing,
And crying
Can I really do before enough
Really IS enough?
Is enough EVER enough?
Of course, I, and everyone around him,
Want him to succeed.
But doesn't he need to want it for himself
In order for everything
To work?
I feel helpless.
And hopeless.
All I can do is continue to smile,

PHIYAH PHLOW

And like the posts,
And comment with my expressions of joy
For all of my friend's children's awesome accomplishments,
Because I am genuinely happy to see these
Posts of Praise.
It gives me hope that our battle
Just might not be over.
Because you see, regardless of what the statistics may say,
The odds really are STILL in his favor..

SPACE AND OPPORTUNITY

A year and 9 months
Approximately 88 weeks of willing myself
To love you
638 days of trying my damnedest to be excited about
Our ongoing union
Roughly 15,341 hours of seeing how well you seem to interact with others
And wondering why you and I never shared that same camaraderie
920,070 minutes of believing that today will FINALLY be THE DAY
That I see you in a far different light and actually WANT to be with you
402,359, 400 seconds sounds like A LOT of time to spend
Working on a relationship that I'd already mentally checked out of
See, as the days went by
I stayed because I thought I had to
As the hours dragged on
I stayed because I felt I needed to
As the seconds ticked away
I stayed because, by then, I was already used to you
And I already knew what to expect when it came to you
And I didn't want to have to start over again
But the thing is
I really did want to walk away from you
I talked about leaving you THOUSANDS of times
And Lord KNOWS everything in me was ready to bounce
But still I remained

PHIYAH PHLOW

Telling myself that I didn't want to "jump ship" until
My back-up plans
Had back-up plans
But apparently you saw right through me
No matter how much I tried to show my love for you
By simply "showing up" as was expected of me
The mistakes I continued to make served as proof
That my heart no longer belonged to you
So you released me back into the world
I cried tears of shock….but not in front of you
I couldn't let you see the sadness I felt for what
Could've been
I felt….ashamed
Embarrassed even
That you would have the nerve to put ME out
When it should've been I who walked out on
YOU
Yet…at the same time…I felt an inexplicable peace
Dare I say…I was relieved
I know I could've put forth a far greater effort to do better
And work harder
But I just didn't want to do better
Or work harder
At least….not with you
So thank you for setting me free
You've graciously gifted me the space I need
To pursue the opportunities I want….
My own
402,359, 400 seconds is A LOT of time to spend
Working on a relationship that the mind has already
Checked out of
And I'll never waste THAT kind of time
Again

PHIYAH PHLOW

"TANKA" VERY MUCH

A Compilation of Tanka Pieces
Definition: A Tanka Poem is derived from Japanese culture. It is a 5 line poem totaling 31 syllables. The 1st and 3rd lines consist of 5 syllables; the 2nd, 4th and 5th lines consist of 7 syllables. Similie, metaphor and personification of inanimate objects are other possible characteristics of a typical Tanka piece.

Music loudly plays,
Yet all I hear are our hearts
Beating strong like drums;
Dancing us ever deeper
Into love overflowing.
©May 5, 2014

As you grip these hips,
My soul takes a cosmic trip.
Anticipation
Of fingertips, sips and drips
Of my nectar on your lips.
©May 6, 2014

A symbol of love?
Or merely a distraction
From the lies that lie
Within the walls of your lies?
Just like this rose...love has died.
©May 9, 2014

Heart....what have you done?
Once again you've tangled us
In a web of love,

PHIYAH PHLOW

Lies, hurt and sheer confusion.
Damn…when will you ever learn?
©June 16, 2014

Wrap me in your seas.
Surround me with your waters,
Beautifully strong.
Make me want to drown in you
So you can be my savior.
©June 17, 2014

These words give me life.
Pages turn; characters speak;
I get excited!
Man....what's gonna happen next?
I love getting lost in you.
©June 17, 2014

Beautiful branches.
Deeply rooted family.
All sprung forth from love.
Seeds planted; watered with care,
Now flowers roam round our earth.
©June 25, 2014

As sun turns to moon,
I wonder will I see you
Dancing through my dreams?
Wish I may, oh wish I might
Dream only of you tonight.
©June 25, 2014

Anticipating.
Weak....awaiting your next move.
Will you touch me here?

PHIYAH PHLOW

Even better....touch me there.
Mmmm oh yessss....right there works too!
©June 28, 2014

Fantasies await
Between these all these rumpled sheets.
Ready to dive in
And lose myself in your world
Til this real one reels me back.
©June 29, 2014

Lord, I feel your peace.
I lift my face to your sun,
And your love fills me.
All my troubles disappear,
And I know that all is well.
©July 1, 2014

Wait…what's this I see?
No more rain? Blue skies? Sunshine?
The storm's really gone?
I can really BREATHE again?
Thank you Lord! You've dried my tears!
©July 3, 2014

Sand at our feet;
World at our fingertips.
Oh what a blessing!
We're not just living this life….
We're standing firm…digging deep.
©July 13, 2014

Hmmm…that's interesting.
When you lie, your nose don't grow;
Your skin just falls off.
I feel so sorry for you.

PHIYAH PHLOW

Guess that's Karma for yo ass.
©July 15, 2014

Open wide baby…
Tasty morsels await you,
And it's ALL for you.
One bite of THIS and I swear
You'll NEVER hunger again.
©July 18, 2014

As God has joined us,
Let NO MAN separate us!
We have a purpose!
Unity….not just a noun,
But a cry for action….NOW!
©August 20, 2014

Man….I'm soooo hungry!
I know just what I want though.
Some you on whole wheat.
You on the side. To drink….you.
And dessert? Why…YOU of course!
© October 24, 2014

Animal instinct
Has taken over my soul.
I apologize
For what's about to happen.
You've brought out the beast in me.
© October 25, 2014

THE GRASS AIN'T ALWAYS GREENER

My man bought me yet another gift today....
A $200 pair of Donna Karans.
You know...the sunglasses?
Yeah...he does that sometimes.
Actually he does that A LOT.
Just buys me expensive gifts out the clear, blue sky.
My girlfriends...I see the slight twinge of green undertones protruding from their pores.
They see me in yet ANOTHER new exclusively designed dress;
Stomping the pavement in yet ANOTHER new pair of Red Bottoms;
Rocking yet ANOTHER new piece of ice in my ears;
On my wrists;
Around my neck.
Never a hair out of place.
Makeup always beat to perfection.

They tell me they wish their men were like mine...
And all I do is smile and shrug off the ignorance of their covetousness.

You see,

They don't know that the exclusive designer dresses perfectly mask the exclusive designer bruises that cover my back.

They don't know that the Red Bottoms hide the red bottoms of my feet....as I was made to stand in a tub

PHIYAH PHLOW

of crushed glass for an hour as penance for his SUSPICION of my cheating.

They have no clue that the ice that covers my ears, wrists, fingers and neck are nothing more than a mere upgrade from the ice that I use to cool his crushing blows.

If they only knew what I went through on the daily, they would know that I only rock the best weaves that money can buy to hide the obvious patches where my natural hair has been ripped from my scalp.

My makeup stays "beat" to hide each and every beating he lays upon my face.

Yes it's true...
I got more clothes
And shoes
And jewelry
And purses
And weave
And bullshit than you can swing a fucking stick at.

But instead of me packing up and leaving, clothed in nothing but the last shred of dignity I have left,

I continue to suck it up, keep smiling at my girlfriends' envy and anticipate the next swing of the stick,

And the goodies it'll net me...

PHIYAH PHLOW

THE QUEEN BEAST HAS SPOKEN

Hmm...
So I see the party started without me
The last thing anybody wanna do is doubt me
Talk all the shit you want but you need to understand
That I bring Fiyah and Desiyah when this pen's in my hand
It ain't enough for me write it
I have to spit it then ignite it
Since lyrical arson ain't a crime
I know I'll NEVER be indicted

Match struck....did I light it?
Beast Battle....try to fight it!
Feelin' weak....awww you slighted?
Bite my shit....I dare you to try it!

See it'll be in your best interest
To stop underestimating me
Because try as you might
You'll never get the best of me
Why you hating?
Quit debating
Trying to kill the quest in me
I've long since graduated
So why you wan' keep testing me?

Man enuffa this shit
It's as simple as this
If you get what you pay for
Then you'll NEVER afford this
I could go on and on for days

PHIYAH PHLOW

But this assassination is done
Just know I may got 99 problems
But lack of "Phlow" DEFINITELY ain't one!

THEM

How dare you turn me into one of "them"
One of "them" lost women who once had a mind of her very own
But who'd now rather put up with bullshit than face the prospect of being forever alone
Inside a weak little girl...making believe that she's full grown

How could you turn me into one of "them"
One of "them" mind-boggled chicks, constantly crazed and obsessin'
Always cryin' and stressin'
Heart breakin' with each new confession
Once considered myself a Queen
Now you got me feelin' "less than"

What did I do to you to make you turn me into one of "them"
One of "them" type females me and my girls used to talk shit about
One who accepts the excuses and foolishness rather than throw his no-good ass out
Funny how quickly self-confidence can be diminished into shame and self-doubt

Why was I so willing to allow you to turn me into one of "them"
Was it the promises you made
Was it that good dick you laid
The fact that you keep all the bills paid
Or maybe I'm just plain ol' afraid

I don't wanna be myself and the pickings out here are few

PHIYAH PHLOW

You know how hard it is being single when everybody's boo'd up but you
So you keep hanging in there, praying he'll change cuz....what else can you really do

So I'll thank y'all kindly not to judge me
Making me feel worse than I already am
Y'all can say whatever the hell you like because at this point, I no longer give a damn
Yeah I'm sure you see me as one of "them" pitiful chicks
But hey....at least I can say I got a man

PHIYAH PHLOW

THIS CHICK HERE

(A Rondel Poem)

So many lines define this body of mine
Roads have been harried...yet I travel on
Giving my all til the day I am gone
Far from perfection....but I'm doing just fine

So many times I've prayed for a sign
Am I doing my best as I journey along?
So many lines define this body of mine
Roads have been harried...yet I travel on

Lost a lot of loves...still I continue to cross that line
Refusing to settle....yet not settling to remain alone
Hoping to one day find this love of my own
No more inhibitions....wouldn't that be divine?

So many lines define this body of mine

PHIYAH PHLOW

TIL HER VERY LAST BREATH

Damn what WAS her name?
Was it Tiffany or Jayne?
Was she loving and supportive?
Or did she constantly lash out in pain?

Did she do everything she could
To be part of the common good?
Did she do things because she WANTED to
And not simply because she SHOULD?

Did she speak life in every ear
Whether or not they chose to hear?
Did she sincerely reciprocate each hug?
Sincerely wiped away each tear?

Was she always as strong as people perceived her to be?
Never too weak to stare adversity down
Was she always wearing the proper shoes
When it came to stomping Satan to the ground?

She was definitely all woman
That you can believe
One never nervous
To drape her heart 'cross her sleeve

She was your mother
Your daughter
Your sister
Your friend
And you'll always remember these pieces of her
In every piece she allowed to spill from her pen..

PHIYAH PHLOW

TIME WELL SPENT

These moments we share
Away from the world, away from prying eyes
Where the only sounds that break the silence
Are our heartbeats and contented sighs

Bring me pleasure immeasurable
And I find myself counting the ways
That I can squeeze another second out of every possible minute
And add 24 more hours to these special days

In this whole grand space time continuum
Did our souls fleetingly touch in each other's dreams
Because it truly blows my mind how we've found in each other
A connection that keeps us joined at the seams

So despite the circumstances that keep us apart
Let's just enjoy these brief moments together
Because until we both make some very pertinent decisions
The next time we touch each other....may be never

PHIYAH PHLOW

TONIGHT

Feeling a little giddy
I haven't partied like this in a while
Nor have I drunk like this in a while
I don't do clubs
I can definitely be a bit of a homebody when I wanna be
So I'm pretty sure it's this crowd
And all these bodies mashed up on this small-ass dance floor
DJ playing suggestive music
Slow music
Slow whine music
Slow whine, bump and grind music
Slow whine, bump and grind your dick on my ass
Music
Damn
Do you have something in your pocket
Or are you just happy to be all up on this ass like that
Probably both
I hope it's both
Especially the former
Mmm mm my gawd what the hell made me wear this dress
With no damn draws
I can feel every inch
Every vein
Every molecule
Of this dude's desire on me
He dancing like he sexin
I wonder if he sexes like he dances
He smells sooooooooo daaaaaaaaaamn gooooooooood
And he's got his lips pressed against my neck

PHIYAH PHLOW

Like he just knew that was…like…that was...
Oh shit…that's my fuckin spot
He's rubbing his hands up and down my thighs
Coming heart-stoppingly close to tracing
The outline of my throbbing triangle
What's going to happen when this song finally stops
Shit….he's got me dripping while we're still vertical
So it's inevitable that the dams will obviously break free soon as he gets me horizontal
That is
If we end up horizontal
Should I even want us to end up horizontal
Because this is so NOT lady-like behavior
I really must stop this
I'm a grown ass
40 year old woman
And I'm up here
Slow whining
Bumping and grinding my ass
On this dude's thickness
Like I'm horny or something
Which, for the record, I am
I can see his face in the mirror as we dance
He looks to be at least 10 years younger than me
Should I really care how old he is though
I mean we're both grown
We're both out here to have a good time
No pre-conceived notions
No hopes
No wishes
No dreams of what this could possibly be
Because obviously
We're both anxious to see
If all the shit we both just spit in our poetry
Is truth

PHIYAH PHLOW

The music stops
My nipples get stiffer
His member grows thicker
And he presses his lips to my ear and whispers
"Wussup?"
I give him a smirk
Glance over at my friends
And mouth the words
"Don't judge me…"

PHIYAH PHLOW

UNSPOKEN

Once upon a midnight lonely
While I thought about you only
Reading many a long and serious letter
I've received from you
As I read them, my eyes crying
My heart's broken, damn near dying
Cuz it thinks that you've been lying
Lying to it all these years
Yes it knows that you've been lying
Lying to it all these years
Now I wipe away my tears

      As I sit there, my mind dazin
      I see nothing, my eyes glazin
      And my feelings are amazin
      Cuz I don't know why they're there
      I really wish I was still with you
      But with all the hurt I've been through
      All the pain and heartaches too
      Could I go through that again
      All the bullshit and different women
      Could I survive all that again
      What do I really have to gain

And then I realize I don't need you
I don't want you, I don't miss you
There's no way that I could go through
All the things I have before
Some things just go best unspoken
This relationship is broken
I've been treated like some token

PHIYAH PHLOW

And I ain't taking it no more
I refuse to be your hobby
So I'm walking out the door
To be seen forever no more..

PHIYAH PHLOW

WHY NOT

A Double Etheree Poem

Yes
It's you
Who has me
Feeling something
So unfamiliar
Just don't want to call it
That little 4-letter word
But why should I lie to myself
When my heart knows how it really feels
So what am I supposed to do with this
Been down this road many times before
Afraid of being hurt again
Yet there's something about you
That eases all my fears
So I close my eyes
Open my heart
And decide
To say
Yes

Challenge Day 16: National Poetry Month

YOU GO GURL!

Hmm....
Could it be I was wrong
We're not all the same
We're not all bitchy
We're not all vain
We don't all gossip
Or start unnecessary mess
We don't all act stink
When we see our sisters being blessed
We're not all out to take
The next one's man
We're not all out to take
The next one's plan
We don't all throw dirt
And then hide our hands
Most of us actually support each other
As much as we can
Most of us give love
Hope and uplifting
Caring and kindness
And mind our own business
A shoulder to cry on
And credit where it's due
And for that, I really want to say
THANK YOU
To all my sisters who have joined me
In breaking the mold
And believing in each other
Regardless of what we've been told
About "how we black women KNOW we can be"

PHIYAH PHLOW

I know we've ALL been skeptical of each other
Because of what we sometimes see
We're already a double minority
In this world
So no need to add to it with the
Side-eyes and insults we hurl
So I love you my sisters
And my words ring true
Keep doing unto me
So I can keep doing unto you
And as long as we continue
To be each other's inspiration
We'll be stronger in solidifying
Our nation

PHIYAH PHLOW

YOU KNOW YOU LOVE MY HAIR

She's survived ponytails
And afro puffs
Shirley Temple Curls
And barrettes and stuff
Saturday morning hot combs
For Sunday School
That feel of heat on ya "kitchen"
That was never cool
Then came the Jheri Curl
With the Jheri Curl drip
And the "kssshhh kssshhh" sound
Falling from every lip
Don't forget the Salt-n-Pepa
And the T-Boz cut
Oh, and the Patra braids
Hanging down to our butt
Halle Berry had us in
The salon from sun up to down
To make sure our 'do was laid
And turnin' heads around town
From glued tracks to sew-ins
To finger waves to pin curls
From French rolls to pinned-up buns
And all us "au naturale" girls
With our "TWA's"
And our big ass 'fros
From 2-strand twists to dreadlocks
Man ANYTHING goes
From cornrows to "Celie" braids
From the 27-Piece to the fresh cold Fade
From 1B/30 to the Brazilian Blowout
Throw on a Lace Front Wig when we want to show
out

PHIYAH PHLOW

From our various textures
To the colors we RAWK
We sistas wear the crowns
That make many mouths drop
So talk all the shit you want about it
But the reason you stop and stare
Is because as much as you hate to admit it

YOU KNOW YOU LOVE MY HAIR

PHIYAH PHLOW

Dedication

If you've ever shown any kind of love to me;
Told me I could be whatever I so chose;
Made me feel that even if I didn't win,
There's still no way I could ever lose.
Ever told me I was the ish and nothing but;
Ever told me I was hardcore down to the core;
Ever helped me climb through an open window As a means of overcoming a shut door;
Ever made me laugh til my stomach hurt Or cry til snot ran out my nose;
Ever held my hand when I needed a friend Or drifted beside me whichever way the wind blows...
This book is dedicated to you And all that you are to me
And I pray that you feel every bit of my soul And my heart in this poetry...

I love you!

Phiyah Phlow

About The Author

Tiffany D. Glover, aka Jayne Phlow, has been writing poetry for roughly 25 years and performing for approximately 17 years. Growing up as an only child, Tiffany retreated into her own private world of imaginary friends and books upon books upon books.

English, Spelling, Grammar and Literature were always her favorite subjects in school and she soon discovered she had a knack for essay writing, entering and actually winning a few contests throughout her middle and high school years.

When artists Lauryn Hill, Alanis Morrisette, Erykah Badu and Jill Scott hit the music scene, she was intrigued at how they sang about their loves and hurts and pains, yet made it sound like sweet therapeutic release. She very quickly followed their leads and too began channeling all of her hurts, pains, aggravations, tears and yes, even love here-and-there, into poetry. Anything that Tiffany was unable to find the courage to SPEAK easily poured out of her pen, generating years upon years of notebook upon notebook packed full of her soul.

After sitting on all of these notebooks for far too long, she finally listened to the urgings of her family and friends and compiled some of her writings into her very first published book of poetry, "Get a Grip: Spilled Ink from my Soul," released February 14, 2014. Get a Grip is a searing collection of 30 very grimy, very raw, very REAL poems, the majority of which are based on specific situations, trials and tribulations that she has had to endure throughout her life thus far. "This is so NOT your friendly, neighborhood, happy poetry," she explains. "Life is not always cute. Some of the moments I chose to write about weren't cute. So I couldn't be cute in penning it. You may not be able to relate to EVERY poem in my book, but I guarantee you'll relate to AT LEAST one."

Jayne Phlow is a contributing writer for BlaqRayn Publishing Plus' BRPP Magazine, an online magazine promoting all forms of artistic expression, where she writes a monthly column titled "Mamas Makin' Moves," which spotlights mothers, and women in general, making big moves in their careers and communities. She's also earned editor credits on two recently released autobiographies and she continues to hone her editing skills through working on other authors' works of fiction, non-fiction and poetry.

She is currently working on her second book of poetry, titled "Phiyah Phlows: Finga Snaps, Hand Claps and Toe Taps," to be tentatively released around the first of the year, and she regularly performs at various open mics, poetry showcases, empowerment conferences and other events throughout her hometown of Charleston, SC and beyond.

She is a single mother to her 15 year-old son, T'Zhean, and is also a recent graduate of Springfield College's School of Human Services, where she obtained her Master's degree in

Community Counseling Psychology. She hopes to some day use her degree, combined with her love of poetry, spoken word and travel, to empower women battling self-esteem issues to transition themselves from emotionally debilitating relationships.

PHIYAH PHLOW

www.ingramcontent.com/pod-product-compliance
Lightning Source LLC
Chambersburg PA
CBHW031402040426
42444CB00005B/385